PEOPLE WHO MADE HISTORY IN
ANCIENT GREECE

by Nicola Morgan

Illustrated by Christa Hook

HODDER
Wayland

an imp[...] Books

© 2000 White-Thomson Publishing Ltd

Produced for Hodder Wayland by
White-Thomson Publishing Ltd
2/3 St. Andrew's Place
Lewes
BN7 1UP

People who made history in

Ancient Greece • Ancient Egypt • Ancient Rome • Native America

Translation from *Odyssey* (page 9) © Dr Philip de Souza

Series concept: Alex Woolf
Editor: Liz Gogerly
Cover Design: Jan Sterling
Inside Design: Stonecastle Graphics Ltd
Mapwork: Peter Bull

Published in Great Britain in 2000 by Hodder Wayland, a division of
Hodder Children's Books.
This edition published in 2001.

The right of Nicola Morgan to be identified as the author and
Christa Hook as the illustrator of this Work has been asserted by
them in accordance with the Copyright, Designs and
Patents Act 1988

A Catalogue record for this book is available from the British Library.

ISBN 07502 3249 8

Printed and bound in Italy by G. Canale & C. S.p.A.

Hodder Children's Books
A division of Hodder Headline Limited
338 Euston Road, London NW1 3BH

Picture acknowledgements
The publisher would like to
thank the following for their
kind permission to use these
pictures:
Ronald Sheridan, Ancient Art
and Architecture Collection Ltd
21, 23, 38; A.K.G Photo, London
6, 12, 16, 21, 25, 26, 29 30, 34
(top and bottom), 37, 40, 41, 42;
The Bridgeman Art Library/
Louvre, Paris/Giraudon 10/
Chartres Cathedral/Giraudon
17; C.M Dixon 12; E.T. Archive 9,
28, 32; Hodder Wayland 5, 22,
30, 33; Michael Holford 8, 18, 24,
43; Ann Ronan at Image Select
14; Scala 36, 43; Tony Stone
front cover (background);
Wellcome Institute 33

Contents

Who were the ancient Greeks?

THE ANCIENT Greeks created a powerful and exciting civilization over 2000 years ago. Ancient Greek civilization started in about 800 BC and flourished until the Romans conquered it in 146 BC, but its importance lasted for much longer.

was successful

At its height, ancient Greece covered most of the map below. Yet the importance of ancient Greece is not about how much land it covered but about what was achieved in knowledge, science, art, literature, architecture, technology and politics.

One way of understanding a civilization is to look at the individuals who made important discoveries or affected the lives of ordinary people. These men and women might have been politicians, architects, scientists, poets or playwrights. For some of these people, we have only a few reliable details about their personal lives but it is what they achieved which is so interesting and important.

How do we know about the ancient Greeks?

We have a great deal of information about the ancient Greeks which has been pieced together from various sources. Archaeologists have dug up buildings and found items used by the people of that time. Archaeologists have also discovered pottery and vases which the ancient Greeks began writing on from about 800 BC onwards. Putting this all together with information from contemporary writers, including Herodotus, Thucydides and Polybius, and also later writers, we can build up a strong picture of what happened during this exciting time.

ATHENS – THE KEY TO ANCIENT GREECE

At the height of its power Athens was one of the most powerful and influential cities in the ancient world. Athens dominated Greece after the wars against Persia, (490–479 BC). Much of what we know about the ancient Greeks today is based on what we have discovered about this great city.

▲ A vase showing a man reciting poetry. Even when writing was invented, people relied on telling and listening to stories recited from memory.

Ancient Greece in the time of Homer

WE KNOW little about Greece before 800 BC mainly because there is very little written down. Archaeologists have discovered the ruins of older palaces and these help us guess about earlier life in Crete and Mycenae. By 1100 BC, these civilizations had fallen, destroyed by earthquake and war. From then until about 800 BC, we talk about the Dark Age, because we know so little.

We believe that all the earliest poetry was oral, recited by travelling bards, who told poetic stories of gods and heroes. Nothing was written down until the Greeks developed a proper alphabet around 800 BC, borrowing the Phoenician alphabet and adding vowels.

The first poetry tells of a mythical age of heroes, when people believed that gods walked amongst humans. Archaeologists have found evidence of some of the places mentioned in these stories, such as Troy and Mycenae, but we can never know how much is history and how much is myth.

▲ Bronze model of a singer playing a lyre, from the eighth century BC. Music was an important accompaniment to poetry.

STORIES ABOUT GODS AND HEROES

Gods and heroes are central to Greek myth and early history. Gods could be proud and cruel. Heroes were proud and cruel too, especially defending their honour. Heroes didn't mind dying young, as long as they had lived with honour. If you showed disrespect for a hero he would have to punish you.

HOMER

poet
circa 800–700 BC

Two of the most famous works of literature ever written were by a man who possibly never existed. Some people believe Homer was several people; some say he was a woman; others deny he existed at all. We will never know for certain. However, most historians believe that Homer was a travelling poet, or bard, and that he was probably blind.

Whoever he was, or wasn't, we talk about Homer as the writer of the *Iliad* and the *Odyssey*, two epic poems which are the first known European literature. Some people even think the Greek alphabet was invented especially to record these two great poems.

▼ Homer, the bard who inspired centuries of writers with his epic poems of gods, heroes and people – the *Iliad* and the *Odyssey*.

SPOTLIGHT ON HOMER

Name:	Homer
Nick-name:	The Poet
Dates:	Nobody knows, but probably during 800–700 BC
Born:	Probably Asia Minor (Turkey)
Job:	Bard
Wrote:	*Iliad, Odyssey, Battle of the Frogs* and *Mice*
Favourite words:	'Rosy-fingered dawn' and 'wine-dark sea'
Quote:	'Always to be the best, distinguished above the rest'
The Greeks believed:	He was blind which may have been untrue
Famous fans:	Alexander the Great used to carry his copy of Homer's work to war

The ancient Greeks certainly believed in Homer's existence and were extremely proud of him. They liked poems which described the age of heroes and they also enjoyed Homer's powerful and beautiful language.

Homer's great poems

• The *Iliad*. Twenty-four books, each with several hundred lines, tell of a few days in the ten-year Trojan War. Whether or not this war really happened, the *Iliad* was an important tale to the ancient Greeks, especially since they won. It is an exciting story full of blood-thirsty descriptions of battles and spears piercing bodies.

• The *Odyssey*. Another twenty-four books, describing parts of Odysseus' delayed journey home after the war. His journey takes nine years.

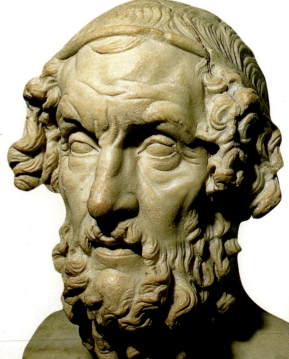

▼ This sculpture of a blind Homer was probably made in the second century AD.

THE ODYSSEY

The opening lines of the *Odyssey* by Homer

'Sing to me, muse, of the man of many talents, who travelled far and wide after he had destroyed the holy city of Troy. Many were the men whose cities he saw, and whose thoughts he came to know. Many were the sorrows his heart endured across the seas, as he struggled to preserve his life and those of his companions.'

It would take twenty-four hours to read the *Iliad* and *Odyssey* aloud. It is difficult to imagine that these were the stories recited from a mixture of memory and invention by travelling bards.

Over 2,500 years later, we still read and study Homer's works. As well as being exciting adventures, the *Iliad* and the *Odyssey* give us another glimpse of the ancient Greek world. The tales are thrilling, funny, sad and sometimes read like fairy tales, but the people and events Homer describes often seem real and true to life.

▼ The Douris Cup. A scene from the *Iliad* with the heroes Hector and Ajax fighting at Troy, each helped by a god – Apollo and Athena.

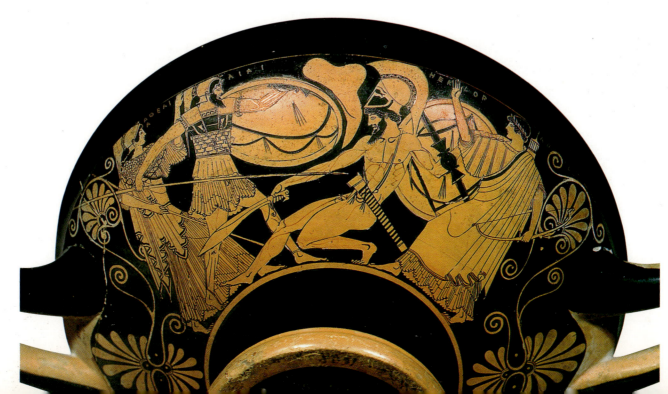

Ancient Greece in the time of Sappho

SAPPHO LIVED during the Archaic period of ancient Greece. By 594 BC a ruler called Solon was transforming life in Athens. When he came to power he tried to help the poor by cancelling any debts they had. He created a system of fair government – these were the first attempts in ancient Greece to build a democracy.

As well as politics the ancient Greeks enjoyed poetry. First there was Homer and the travelling bards who recited oral poetry. By the sixth century BC poetry could be written down and it developed into many different forms, styles and rhythms. Poets themselves were highly respected and were paid for performances – many could earn a good living, much like a singer nowadays.

People believed that each area of life was connected to a different god or goddess. The goddesses of poetry were the Nine Muses, daughters of Zeus, the king of the gods. Poetry included all types of music, singing and drama and a different Muse looked after each.

▼ From a Roman tomb, showing the Nine Muses. Terpsichore is the one holding a lyre.

SAPPHO

Poetess
circa 620–580 BC

We remember Sappho for her beautiful poetry but we know few facts about her. She was born on the island of Lesbos and lived there most of her life. We think she probably came from a rich family because she had plenty of free time to write.

Later in life she was banished from Lesbos to Sicily because she criticized the new ruler, Pittacus, but she returned when he lost power about ten years later.

THE TENTH MUSE

'Some say there are nine Muses: but they are wrong. Look at Sappho of Lesbos; she makes ten.'

Plato said this of Sappho about 200 years after she lived.

The ancient Greeks thought Sappho was a brilliant poet. In those days it was difficult to become a famous writer or poet, especially if you were a woman. Greece was an enormous place and there were no televisions or radios; or printing-machines to make copies of books. Yet Sappho was so admired in her own lifetime that coins were made with her face on. Solon, the Athenian ruler, also tried to learn one of her songs, 'Because I want to learn it and die,' he said.

◄ Sappho, pictured with a lyre, which accompanied lyric poetry.

SPOTLIGHT ON SAPPHO

Name:	Sappho
Dates:	circa 620–580 BC
Born:	Lesbos
Job:	Lyric poet
Family:	Probably married; had a daughter, called Cleis
Personality:	Emotional
Likes:	Flowers, the moon, beautiful people, emotional suffering
Habit:	Poetic exaggeration – claimed that she came close to death as she looked at someone she loved

Sappho's poetry

Sappho wrote lyric poetry, which was accompanied by an instrument called a lyre. We still talk about the 'lyrics' of a song. Lyric poetry describes topics like love, hate, beauty, flowers, pleasure and sadness. It expresses personal feelings and is quite different from epic poetry.

Sappho wrote nine books of poems altogether, but we only have two poems and some fragments left. Her poems are passionate, beautiful and simple. She invented a new rhythm for verse, called a Sapphic.

◄ Stone bust of Sappho with her name underneath.

A Taste Of Sappho's Love Poetry

Desire grips me yet again
I feel my legs and arms dissolve
It is overtaking me with sweet pain
All I can do is surrender

Sappho was always in love. She addressed many poems to Aphrodite, goddess of love. She was possibly the lover of Alcaeus, another famous lyric poet on Lesbos.

Many of her love poems are for girlfriends. The word lesbian originally meant 'to do with love' because so much love poetry came from Lesbos. The modern meaning came later because of Sappho's love of women. The ancient Greeks were quite open about homosexuality. But later writers judged her as a dreadful woman with no morals.

There is a story about how she died, which adds to the picture we have of her as a passionate and dramatic woman. It is said that she jumped to her own death from a rock, because the boatman, Phaon, rejected her love. We do not know what she was really like, but we can enjoy her lovely poetry.

◄ Marble statue of Venus, the Roman goddess of love, copied from the Greek original of Aphrodite, who inspired Sappho's poetry.

Ancient Greece in the time of Pythagoras

AFTER SOLON'S death in about 560 BC, Athens was ruled by Peisistratus. Although Peisistratus was called 'tyrant', he continued to improve life for many people. He encouraged art and literature and united many parts of Greece. By 508 BC, Kleisthenes had taken control of Athens and made reforms to the constitutional structure. Meanwhile, the whole of Greece was under continued threat from the mighty Persian Empire.

Major discoveries were also being made in mathematics and astronomy. Without clocks or calendars, watching the stars and planets helps people understand time and seasons. However, to do astronomy properly, you need mathematics.

The Egyptians were advanced mathematicians long before the Greeks, but, as far as we know, Egyptians focused on questions like how? or what? rather than why? A Greek mathematician called Thales (circa 640–550 BC) visited Egypt and brought this practical knowledge to Greece. Thales' studies were also very useful: he predicted a solar eclipse in 585 BC, calculated the number of days in a year, and worked out the lengths of the seasons.

► This picture from the sixteenth century AD shows Thales' view of a flat earth floating on water. It shows earth, water, air and fire, from which many Greeks believed everything was made.

PYTHAGORAS
Mathematician and philosopher circa 560–495 BC

Pythagoras was absolutely passionate about his subject, mathematics. He loved the subject so much that he opened a school but could only find one pupil. He paid the pupil to stay, giving him money for each new rule he learnt. The pupil was soon enjoying himself so much that when Pythagoras threatened to leave, the pupil paid Pythagoras to stay, giving him money for each new rule he taught.

Pythagoras later set up a successful school in Italy. Everyone came to his lectures, including women, although they were not allowed to attend places of learning. Pythagoras married one of his female followers, the beautiful and intelligent Theano. Pythagoras' pupils called themselves the Order of the Pythagoreans.

'The most noble philosopher among the Greeks'.

Herodotus (485-425 BC), the first Greek historian, said this about Pythagoras.

▼ Pythagoras, brilliant mathematician and religious mystic.

What did Pythagoras find out?

Pythagoras and his followers discovered many things about maths and astronomy, including:

• fractions
• odd and even numbers
• musical intervals
• square numbers, triangular numbers and the patterns surrounding them
• the earth is spherical
• the planets, moon and stars revolve in two ways

What did Pythagoras believe?

• **Religion:** Pythagoreans believed that a person's soul is immortal. If a man behaved well, his soul would return as a noble person. If he behaved badly, he would return as a pig, dog, or woman. Since any animal might contain the soul of a dead friend, Pythagoreans were vegetarian.

• **Health:** Pythagoreans followed peculiar rules for a healthy body and soul. A rule about not eating beans has an amusing possible explanation: soul was like wind, so anything which caused wind should be avoided, in case part of the soul escaped.

• **Mathematics:** Pythagoreans believed that mathematics was the only way to purify the soul, so they did as much of it as they possibly could.

▶ A fifteenth century picture of Pythagoras working out musical notes using bells and containers of water.

SPOTLIGHT ON PYTHAGORAS

Name:	Pythagoras
Dates:	circa 560–495 BC
Born:	Samos
Married:	Theano
Secret symbol:	☆
Big mistake:	Thought the Sun went round the Earth
Biggest extravagance:	So delighted when he discovered his Theorem that he sacrificed 100 oxen — hoping that they did not contain the souls of 100 friends
Famous fans:	Albert Einstein (AD 1879–1955) needed Pythagoras' Theorem for his own discoveries

RULES OF THE PYTHAGOREANS

Don't eat beans; don't walk in the main street; don't stir fire with iron; don't touch a white cockerel; don't eat a heart; don't stand on nail-clippings; don't leave an impression of your body on the bed when you get up; rub out traces of pot ashes in fire-place; help a man loading but not unloading; don't look in a mirror by a lamp.

▲ A stone carving of Pythagoras hard at work.

Although Pythagoras is associated with some strange beliefs he is most famous for Pythagoras' Theorem, which school children still learn today during their mathematics lessons. But the most important thing he did was to use mathematics to prove ideas and show why things are as they are.

Ancient Greece in the time of Aeschylus

IN 490 BC the Persians attempted to invade Marathon in Attica. The Athenians had to take the Persians on alone. Against all odds the Athenians won the battle of Marathon, but ten years later the Persians were back. They beat the Greeks in 480 BC at the Battle of Thermopylae.

The Persian victory was shortlived though; many Athenians moved to the island of Salamis and together with other Greeks plotted the downfall of the Persians. Later in 480 BC, the Greeks defeated the Persian fleet at the battle of Salamis, and in 479 they ended the threat by defeating the Persian army at Plataea.

The Greeks used drama to tell their stories of gods, heroes and people. When we talk of Greek drama, we usually mean tragedy. Tragic plays began in the 6th Century BC, with the poet Thespis. Thespis used one actor in his plays.

▼ The theatre at Delphi, dating from the time of Aeschylus. Sitting anywhere in the audience, you could hear an actor whispering.

Tragedy meant something particular to the Greeks. The play had to be about important people and ideas, not everyday occurrences. The main character had to be a noble person who either made one bad choice or had a character flaw which led him to do something dishonourable.

AESCHYLUS

The First Great Playwright
circa 525–456 BC

Aeschylus was not only a playwright, but also a soldier who fought at the Greek victories of Marathon and Salamis. One of his first plays was *The Persians*, which celebrates the achievements of the Athenians and other Greeks over their mighty enemy. Aeschylus must have been proud of his fighting, as he asked to be remembered as a soldier from Marathon, not a writer.

Aeschylus was successful as a playwright, winning many drama competitions. Even after his death he continued to win competitions. The government had passed a law which allowed the actors from the chorus of Aeschylus' plays to be paid from government money, which was a great incentive.

DRAMA COMPETITIONS

Religious festivals in ancient Greece were also a time to have fun. People enjoyed processions and drama competitions and they travelled from all over the Greek-speaking world to visit the Great Dionysia festival. The works of famous playwrights were performed then judged. The winner was crowned with ivy and the victory was probably followed by parties to celebrate.

► Aeschylus, holding a mask that an actor would wear on stage. An actor's own facial expression was hard to see from such a distance.

SPOTLIGHT ON AESCHYLUS

Name:	Aeschylus
Nick-name:	Father of Greek tragedy
Dates:	circa 525–456 BC
Born:	Eleusis near Athens
Job:	Playwright, soldier
Appearance:	Completely bald. There is a cruel (and probably untrue) story that he died when an eagle thought his shiny head was a stone and dropped a tortoise on it
Believed:	There is no heaven or hell – you will be punished or rewarded during your lifetime

Aeschylus' plays

Aeschylus wrote about ninety plays; we know the titles of eighty but only seven survive. His plays are quite different from anything which had been done before. For example, he was the first playwright to use a second actor – an idea nobody had tried before. Aeschylus also introduced costumes and scenery, making the plays more exciting.

► Actor's mask for use in tragedy.

His most famous surviving plays are a trilogy called the *Oresteia* which was first performed in 458 BC and is so powerful that it is still acted today. It tells the story of Orestes, who killed his mother, Clytemnestra, because she took a lover and killed Orestes' father, Agamemnon. Orestes is pursued and punished by the Furies, the goddesses of revenge and punishment. By the end of the third play, Orestes has been punished enough and is freed by the court of Athens and Athene, goddess of wisdom. These plays show Aeschylus' interest in justice and mercy, punishment and reward, and how we can become wise through suffering.

▼ A bronze panel showing Orestes killing his mother. Her lover is running away.

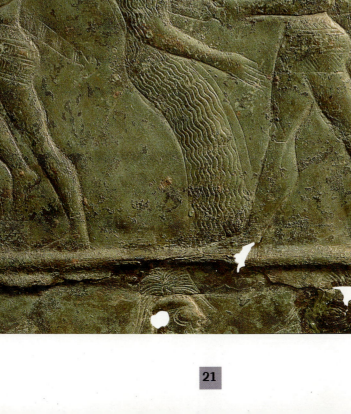

OTHER PLAYWRIGHTS

Sophocles (circa 496–406 BC)
Wrote *King Oedipus, Electra, Antigone*.
Interested in right and wrong. Beautiful poetry.
Very popular.

Euripides (circa 485–406 BC)
Wrote *Medea, The Bacchae*.
Interested in psychology and why people do things.
Popular after his death.

Ancient Greece in the time of Pericles

WHEN PERICLES was born, Greece was made up of lots of city-states all making their own rules. The Greek word for city-state was *polis*, which is where we get our word politics. Athens was the largest city-state, and sometimes the strongest, but there were other powerful city-states, such as Syracuse and Miletos.

Each city-state also had its own type of government. Most were ruled by wealthy families — a government like this was called an aristocracy. Sometimes city-states were governed by a few men and this was called an oligarchy. Some city-states were governed by a king known as a tyrant *(tyrannos)*. In all these types of government, ordinary people had little power. However, from this time, throughout Greece, city-states such as Athens were slowly introducing a form of democracy, or 'rule by the people'. This process was started by Solon and Kleisthenes.

City-states were often at war with each other, and with other countries, such as Persia. When Pericles was a child, Athens was in the middle of the terrible war with Persia. When Pericles was about 15, in 480 BC, the Greeks beat the Persians at the Battle of Salamis.

▼ This pot shows Greek citizens casting votes, watched over by the gods, including Athena, goddess of wisdom and justice.

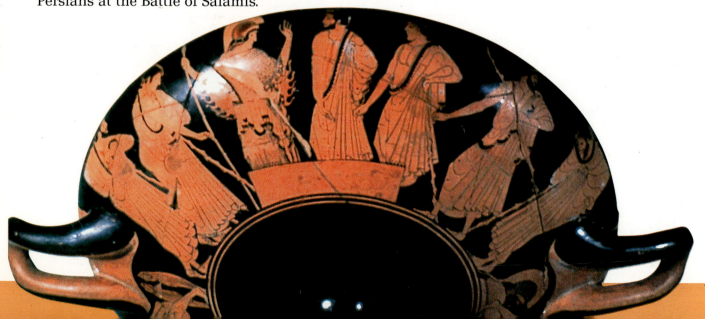

PERICLES
Politician
circa 495–429 BC

Pericles was re-elected to lead Athens nearly every year from 461 BC to his death in 429 BC. He kept control mainly because he was a brilliant speaker, a strong leader and gave people what they wanted, such as paid jobs, free entertainment and beautiful buildings.

As leader of the ruling Democratic party, Pericles changed many aspects of Athenian life. He introduced payments for members of the Assembly, so people no longer needed to be rich to play a part in politics. He spread power more widely, although women and slaves still had no power.

PERICLES' WISDOM

On a ship when the helmsman (steering-person) was frightened by an eclipse of the sun, Pericles held his cloak over the man's eyes and asked him whether this was frightening. When the man said, 'Of course not,' Pericles answered, 'So what's the difference between this and an eclipse, except that an eclipse is caused by something bigger than my cloak?'

Pericles used his own power over other city-states in more dishonest ways. During the war with Persia, the Delian League had been formed by Athens and other city-states so they were more of a mighty force against the Persians. After the war with the Persians ended in 449 BC, Pericles continued to take money from his old allies for the war effort. Eventually there was lots of money saved and no war to spend it on. Pericles forced his allies to let him use much of this money to improve Athens.

► Pericles making a speech. His brilliance at speaking saved the life of Aspasia, his mistress, after she had been sentenced to death.

SPOTLIGHT ON PERICLES

Name:	Pericles
Nick-name:	The Olympian
Dates:	circa 495–429 BC
Born:	Athens
Family:	Educated, wealthy
Married:	Separated from Athenian wife; had famous mistress, Aspasia
Hobbies:	Making speeches, commanding warships, going to plays written by famous friends, spending other people's money on buildings
Personality:	Never went to dinner with anyone in case they thought he was favouring them

Pericles' achievements

Pericles was responsible for rebuilding Athens after its war with Persia. He ordered the construction of many buildings and temples, some of which can still be seen today. The most impressive and famous is the Parthenon, a huge temple on the Acropolis, a hill in the middle of Athens. Some people, perhaps jealous of his popularity, criticized Pericles for spending so much public money on huge buildings, and also for holding expensive festivals.

◄ Aspasia, a noble woman from Miletus who was Pericles' mistress. The Athenians disliked her, partly because she had so much influence.

▲ Pericles is usually shown wearing a helmet. The story is that he had an odd-shaped skull. One writer said it was big enough to fit eleven sofas inside!

The years when Pericles was in power were called the Golden Age of Athens. This period of wealth and success began to fade in 431 BC when the Peloponnesian War against Sparta began – Athens eventually lost in 404 BC. No sooner had this war started than a dreadful plague hit Athens. A year later, in 429 BC, Pericles died of a fever.

ATHENS – THE PLACE TO BE SEEN

Pericles encouraged artists, sculptors, actors, musicians, writers, scientists and thinkers to come to Athens. It must have been a lively place, and certainly the place to be if you wanted to see the newest play or hear the cleverest speakers talking about exciting scientific ideas.

▼ The Parthenon, a temple to Athena, overlooking Athens. Built by Iktinos and Kallicrates on the order of Pericles.

Ancient Greece in the time of Socrates

BETWEEN 431 BC and 404 BC Athens was at war with another city-state called Sparta. This was called the Peloponnesian War. In 404 BC the Spartans beat the Athenians. However, the Spartans allowed democracy to be re-introduced in Athens in 403 BC.

During this time, Athens remained an important centre of learning and philosophers would come to argue in the agora. Philosophy means love of wisdom, which to the ancient Greeks meant knowledge of all sorts. Ancient Greek philosophers would discuss many things, from what the world was made of to how to behave.

The earliest philosophers focused on how the world works and what it is made of. They are called natural philosophers. They tried to explain everything without using myths: thunder is natural, they said, not Zeus being angry. Later, philosophers focused on how to behave — once again there were many different ideas.

▼ Philosophers discussing their ideas in Aristotle's school of philosophy.

SOCRATES

**Philosopher
circa 469–399** BC

Socrates came from a wealthy Athenian family. He served in the army but spent most of his life talking and listening.

Socrates is one of the most famous philosophers the world has known and he had a huge influence on later philosophers. His reputation for being a kindly intellectual with a good sense of humour meant he was always popular with his circle of friends.

However, people who thought they knew everything would not find Socrates so pleasant. His main opponents were the Sophists, people whose view was, 'It is not possible to know anything, yet I am so wise that I know everything'. The Sophists even charged a fee for listening to them.

SOCRATES' OR PLATO'S IDEAS?

Socrates wrote nothing down. His famous pupil, Plato, wrote his own ideas down as conversations, but some of these ideas could have been Plato's. Even if we do not know Socrates' exact words, we know about his logical mind and his desire always to do right.

▼ Socrates, who searched for the answers to questions like, 'What is beauty?' and 'What is the best way to behave?'.

SPOTLIGHT ON SOCRATES

Name:	Socrates
Nick-name:	Gadfly — because he went round stinging people with his arguments
Dates:	circa 469–399 BC
Born:	Athens
Job:	Putting conceited fools in their places
Appearance:	Ugly, pot-bellied, bulging eyes, snub nose
Family:	Wealthy; mother a midwife, father a sculptor; married Xanthippe when he was 50; had three children
Personality:	Modest — in one of his famous quotes he said, 'The only thing I know is that I know nothing'

His beliefs

Socrates' main aim was to show people that their ideas were wrong. His trick was to pretend that he knew nothing and then start asking clever questions which would make people say the opposite of what they had first said. We now call this 'Socratic argument'. Socrates often made people look foolish in public and for this reason he made many enemies.

Apart from showing weaknesses in other people's arguments, Socrates looked for definitions of things like 'happiness' and 'goodness'.

◄ Wall-painting of Socrates, painted in the first century AD. It shows how unattractive he was.

▶ A painting showing Socrates about to drink the poisonous hemlock.

Although he said he knew nothing, he believed that it was possible to answer everything with pure reason – not through using the senses or by following the rules of society.

Socrates claimed to be guided by an inner voice which always told him what was right. This made his enemies accuse him of listening to false gods.

Socrates was eventually accused of corrupting the young with his ideas, and of worshipping the wrong gods. He refused to change and was found guilty. Socrates could have chosen exile, but he preferred to die for his beliefs. He chose to kill himself by taking hemlock, a deadly poison, to avoid giving his judges the pleasure of executing him.

OTHER ANCIENT GREEK PHILOSOPHERS

Plato (circa 427–347 BC), Socrates' most famous pupil, and a brilliant philosopher himself. Believed that although real things change, 'perfect ideas' do not. Also interested in geometry: said, 'God always does geometry'.

Aristotle (circa 384–322 BC), Plato's most famous pupil. Focused on the study of nature. Did not believe in Plato's 'perfect ideas'.

Ancient Greece in the time of Hippocrates

IN ATHENS and other parts of Greece, people were living through the turmoil of the Persian Wars, the plague in 430 BC and the Peloponnesian War, which Athens lost to Sparta in 404 BC. This time also covered the Golden Age of Pericles, so it was a time of upheaval and great change.

Scientists and philosophers, such as Plato and Aristotle, were slowly discovering more about the world but there was still a great deal of superstition and ignorance.

Fortunately, the Greeks, like other ancient peoples, did also realize that many plants can cure illness and that there are other practical ways of staying healthy, such as eating and exercising sensibly. Successful doctors were important and respected people, and were often very highly paid.

▲ A present to the God of healing, Asclepius, to thank him for making someone's leg better. Greeks believed that the illness was cured if you pleased the gods.

◄ A doctor letting blood out of a patient. Hippocrates' ideas about bleeding patients lasted for hundreds of years – some doctors even do it today!

HIPPOCRATES

Doctor
circa 460–377/359 BC

Hippocrates' life

Very little is known about Hippocrates' life. However, we do know that Hippocrates had his own school of medicine on the island of Cos and the books which we call 'Hippocratic' probably came from the teachings and research from that school.

Even though we know so little about Hippocrates, he is still called the father of medicine. The reason for this is that he was the first recorded person who managed to separate medicine from religion or witchcraft. Disease was part of nature, he said, and could be treated with natural remedies, not miracles. He observed the tiniest details of symptoms and recorded these for other doctors to learn from. Hippocrates also developed rules about how doctors should behave towards patients.

▶ Hippocrates, the doctor who believed that science was the way to cure and prevent disease.

THE HIPPOCRATIC OATH

Modern doctors still have to swear the Hippocratic Oath. This oath, taken from Hippocrates' teachings, describes a doctor's duty never to harm his patient, and to keep secret what his patient tells him.

Ancient Greece in the time of Alexander the Great

WAR BETWEEN each other and against Persia left the city-states of Athens and Sparta considerably weakened. By the fourth century BC Athens was beginning to flourish again but it was no longer in a powerful enough position to unite the Greek city-states and create a Greek empire.

Macedonia was a country to the north of Greece which the Greeks had largely ignored. However, from 359 BC onwards Philip II of Macedon had been building up his country to make it more powerful. He wanted to destroy the mighty Persian Empire and to do this he needed control of Greece. In 338 BC Philip and his army beat the Greek army at the battle of Chaeronea and took over Greece. Less than a year later he was ready to fight against Persia. In Athens, many people did not like being ruled by Macedonians, whom they called 'barbarians'; but they had little choice.

Philip II was Alexander's father and Alexander inherited Philip's desire to beat the Persians and to rule as much of the world as possible.

▼ Gold medallion showing Philip II of Macedon (circa 382–336 BC), father of Alexander the Great.

▼ Detail from a tomb called the Alexander Sarcophagus. It shows a Greek rider, believed to be Alexander, from about 330 BC.

ALEXANDER

**General
circa 356–323 BC**

Alexander expected to excel at everything. Aged 14, he tamed a wild stallion, Bucephalus, after his father said the horse was too wild to ride. His chief private tutor, Leonidas, set harsh standards: he believed that the healthiest breakfast was a walk before dawn, and would check Alexander's bag in case his mother had slipped something tasty into it. Alexander was also taught briefly by Aristotle, though they argued later on – perhaps when Alexander executed Aristotle's nephew Kallisthenes for disagreeing with him.

Alexander was sixteen when he was first left in charge of Macedonia and eighteen when he fought his first battle. Immediately afterwards, he visited Athens for the only time in his life, which is remarkable considering that he became ruler of Greece.

◄ Alexander the Great, the extraordinary young leader who led his army to rule most of the known world.

SPOTLIGHT ON ALEXANDER THE GREAT

Name:	Alexander
Nick-name:	The Great
Dates:	circa 356–323 BC
Born:	Macedon
Parents:	Philip II and Olympias
Job:	King, general
Features:	Muscles, lots of scars
Best friend:	Hephaestion
Horse:	Bucephalus
Wives:	Roxana, Stateira and Parysatis (Polygamy, or marrying more than once, was a Macedonian royal custom)

Alexander became king aged nineteen after his father's assassination. He was thirty-three when he died of a fever, but in those fourteen years he conquered much of the known world, including Persia, Asia Minor, Egypt, and India up to the river Ganges. Here he had to stop because his men refused to go further. He sulked in his tent for days, but eventually agreed to go back.

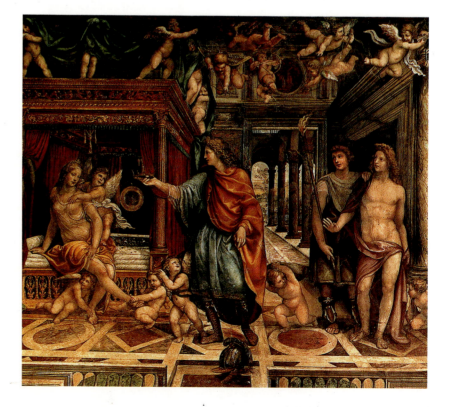

► This Renaissance painting is an interpretation of the marriage of Alexander to Roxana. Alexander admired her great beauty.

◄ This mosaic, called *'The Alexander Battle'*, shows Alexander fighting the Persian king, Darius III, at the Battle of Issos.

Modern historians disagree about whether Alexander just wanted to conquer the world or whether he wanted East and West to live in peace and learn from each other. He was intelligent, brave and brilliant and his soldiers adored him. However, he had a dark side. He killed his own foster brother, Kleitus, in a drunken fight, and burnt down a palace during a party. Sometimes he was accused of not being truly Greek, because he adopted Eastern habits.

Whatever his faults, he succeeded in his mission: to destroy the Persian empire and replace it with a strengthened Greek one.

ALEXANDER'S LOVE OF KNOWLEDGE

Alexander did not always destroy the places he conquered. He loved knowledge, so in many places he created libraries and centres of learning. For example, he created the city of Alexandria, in Egypt, which became a world centre of knowledge for hundreds of years. He also carried a copy of Homer's *Iliad* into every battle.

Ancient Greece in the time of Archimedes

UNDER ALEXANDER the Great, the Greek Empire had spread to new areas, including Asia Minor, Afghanistan, Iraq, Iran, India and Egypt. In all of these lands new cities were formed and the people there adopted many Greek ways, including democracy.

The Greeks also influenced the way people questioned the world around them and then found answers to those questions. The word 'science' comes from the Latin word for 'knowledge'; scientists look for what can be known about the world. They can use what earlier scientists discover, but the earliest Greeks had to start from almost nothing.

At first, philosophy, mathematics, astronomy, nature and all the sciences were mixed together. Early scientists were often wrong but, when you consider how they started from nothing and how little they had in the way of instruments, this is unsurprising. Some of their ideas seem foolish today but our knowledge today comes from hundreds of years of work — the Greeks were a huge part of that work.

► This Roman relief shows a crane, similar to Archimedes' early designs, being used to build the Aterii monument in Rome in the first century BC.

ARCHIMEDES

Scientist
circa 287–212 BC

Archimedes came from an educated family. He was the son of an astronomer, Pheidias, and was related to the king of Syracuse, Hieron II. He was born and lived in Syracuse, though he also studied in Alexandria.

Many of Archimedes' findings have turned out to be right. The sixteenth century scientist, Copernicus, and Galileo in the seventeenth century both used his discoveries. He had the ability to see things in his mind and then to prove them mathematically. This new method of starting with a theory and then setting out to prove it is why he is sometimes called 'the first scientist'.

A few of Archimedes' discoveries:
- understood the principle of levers and pulleys to move huge objects (like a crane)
- calculated areas and volumes
- predicted eclipses, measured distances to stars, made a planetarium, measured the year
- created machines such as the Archimedean Screw which could raise water from a lower level to a higher level

ARCHIMEDES' CLEVER MACHINES

Archimedes was enormously respected, even by his enemies. He designed cranes with mechanical claws which lifted enemy ships out of the water, and catapults which could hurl rocks of 1.5 tons. The Romans would often flee if they saw one of his machines being used against them.

◄ Archimedes, sometimes called 'the first scientist'. He had the ability to visualize scientific principles and make them work.

SPOTLIGHT ON ARCHIMEDES

Name:	Archimedes
Dates:	circa 287–212 BC
Born:	Syracuse (Sicily)
Job:	Scientist
Personality:	Scatty, super-intelligent
Famous fans:	Galileo, Copernicus, Isaac Newton
Quote:	'Give me a firm spot on which to stand and I will move the Earth'
Impressive trick:	Moved a ship over dry land, using one hand and a pulley

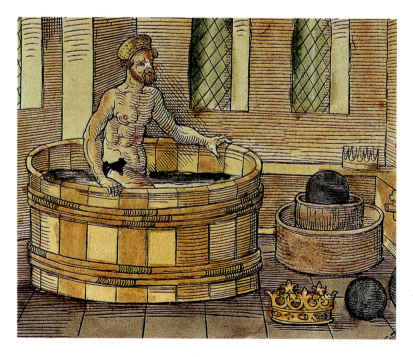

▲ A sixteenth century engraving showing Archimedes in his bath. You can see the crown and weights, as well as a container to collect the overflowed water.

'Eureka'

The most famous story about Archimedes is the *'eureka'* one. Though it is probably not entirely true, it gives us a clue to Archimedes' personality and one of his cleverest discoveries. King Hieron had asked Archimedes to discover whether his jeweller had cheated by making his crown with less gold and more silver. Archimedes puzzled over this in the bath. Observing that his body made the water rise, he realized something amazing. He leapt out and ran naked through the streets excitedly shouting *'eureka!'*, Greek for 'I've found it!'

Archimedes had realized that he could weigh the crown, then find a piece of gold which weighed the same. He could then find out whether the crown was completely made of gold by seeing if each made the same amount of water overflow when placed in a bowl full of water. We believe that the jeweller was guilty but Archimedes would have been much more interested in the scientific principles which he had discovered.

Archimedes died as he had lived: obsessed with his work. When the Romans took control of his home town, Syracuse, he continued to work. When a Roman soldier met him Archimedes refused to move until he had finished a calculation. The soldier, who didn't recognize him, drew his sword and killed him.

▲ A mosaic showing a Roman soldier about to kill Archimedes while he works.

HOMERSAPPHOPYTHAGORASAESCHYLUSPERICLESSOCRATESHIPPOCRATESALEXANDER**ARCHIMEDES**

How did it all end?

DURING THE two hundred years after Alexander the Great, the Romans were growing in strength. They began conquering Greek city-states in Southern Italy. In 168 BC they conquered Macedonia but in 146 BC the Romans conquered the rich Greek city-state of Corinth. Greece was no longer the powerful country it had been.

However, the Romans did not destroy the great culture which they found – they took it for themselves and before long the Romans were learning Greek too. Romans admired and copied Greek architecture, literature, theatre, philosophy and science, and many aspects of their way of life. When the Romans went on to further conquests, they took Greek achievements with them wherever they went. So, even though Greeks ceased ruling themselves, their civilization and achievements continue to be important right up to the present day.

▼ A Roman mosaic from the third century AD, showing a scene from Homer's *Odyssey*: Odysseus being tempted by the Sirens.

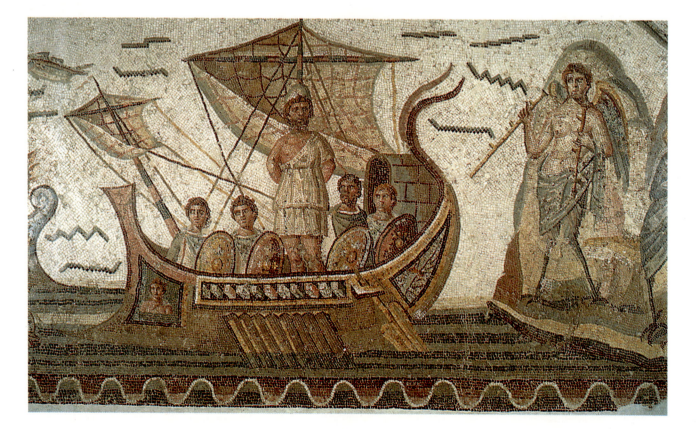

It is amazing to think how much the ancient Greeks continue to influence our lives: democracy is the system of government used in many countries; modern physics and mathematics still use rules discovered by the Greeks such as Thales, Pythagoras and Archimedes; much modern architecture in the cities of Europe and the United States is copied from their buildings; western philosophy is hugely influenced by the works of Socrates, Plato and Aristotle; modern literature is full of references to ancient Greek writers. Western languages, including English, are dotted with ancient Greek words and in schools and universities all over the world people still read ancient Greek literature and even learn their language.

'I say someone in another time will remember us.' Sappho

▲ When Athenians wanted to get rid of a politician they wrote his name on a piece of broken pottery called an 'ostrakon'. The person with the most 'votes' was banished. Today, we use the word 'ostracize' to mean to ignore or shun.

► A vase from the fifth century BC shows a victorious athlete being crowned with a wreath, just as athletes today are awarded prizes or medals at competitions, such as the Olympics.

Timeline

Bronze Age (3000–1100 BC)

3000–1100	Minoan civilization on Crete
	(some palaces destroyed in 1700, possibly by earthquake)
2000	First Greek-speaking people arrive on mainland Greece
1600	Rise of Mycenaean culture on mainland
1200	Possible date of Trojan War. Some Mycenaean palaces fall

Dark Age (1100–800 BC)

by 1100	Mycenaean and Minoan cultures have fallen
900–800	Greeks travel more widely and build Greek city-states in Asia Minor

Archaic Period (800–500 BC)

800	Greeks adapt Phoenician alphabet, introducing vowels
776	First Olympic games
800–700	Probable dates of Homer
750	Greeks continue to expand into Italy and Black Sea area
620–580	Probable dates of Sappho
638–559	Solon
585	Thales (640–550 BC) predicts eclipse of sun
584–495	Probable dates of Pythagoras
545	Persians expand into Greece; Peisistratus tyrant in Athens until 527BC
525–456	Probable dates of Aeschylus
508	Democracy introduced in Athens by Kleisthenes

Classical Age (500–323 BC)

500–449   Persian Wars; Greeks win at Marathon (490 BC) and Salamis (480 BC)
495–429   Probable dates of Pericles
478–432   Athens' greatest period
431–404   Peloponnesian War between Athens and Sparta (Sparta wins)
430   Plague in Athens
469–399   Probable dates of Socrates
359   Philip II becomes king of Macedon
338   Philip II rules Greece as head of League of Corinth
460–377/359 Probable dates of Hippocrates
356–323   Probable dates of Alexander the Great
322   Athenian democracy ends

Hellenistic Period (322–331 BC)

287–212   Probable dates of Archimedes
212   Rome defeats Syracuse and takes over Sicily
211–205   Macedonians at war with Rome (also 202–197 and 171–168)
168   Rome defeats Macedonia
146   Rome defeats Corinth – Greece now ruled by Rome
31   Rome wins battle of Actium – last Hellenistic ruler defeated. Rome now rules Egypt, Macedonia, Greece and much of Europe, Africa and Asia

Glossary

agora — The market-place, where public meetings were often held.

archaeologist — Person whose job is to dig up things from the past.

architecture — Style of buildings.

aristocracy — When power is in the hands of wealthy or important families, from the words *aristos* (best) and *kratos* (power).

aristocrat — A member of one of ruling families.

banished — Sent to another country as a punishment.

barbarians — Originally anyone from the North, or anyone whom the Athenians considered uncivilized because their language sounded like 'bar bar'.

bard — A poet who tells stories using poetry and music.

democracy — In Greek terms this meant allowing the citizens to make their own decisions rather than their leaders.

epic — Long story-poem, about heroes, gods and ancient stories.

Furies — Three frightening half-goddesses whose job was to punish murderers, especially those who murdered a relative; also called the 'Eumenides' or 'Kindly Ones'.

geometry — The mathematics of shapes and angles.

immortal — Never dies.

literature — Written work which represents a particular civilization, including poetry, history, drama.

lyre — Musical instrument like a small harp.

lyric — Type of poetry which is accompanied by a lyre.

myth — Ancient story which does not claim to be true.

mythical — From a myth.

oligarchy — When power is in the hands of a few people, chosen by each other.

oral — Spoken, not written down.

ostracize — To banish a politician after the people have voted to sack him.

philosophy — Love of wisdom — and Greek wisdom included every type of knowledge and enquiry.

playwright — Someone who writes plays.

tragedy — Type of drama; it has an important message about human life but does not always have a sad ending.

trilogy — Three plays making a complete story.

Further information

Pronunciation guide

Emphasize the syllable in bold

Aeschylus	**Ees**-kil-us
Aphrodite	Af-ro-**die**-tee
Archimedes	Ark-im-**eed**-eez
Aristotle	**Ar**-ist-ot-ul
Athene	Ath-**ee**-nee
Kleisthenes	**Klys**-then-eez
Einstein	**Ine**-stine
Euripides	Yur-**ip**-id-eez
Galileo	Gal-ill-**ay**-oh
Heracles	**Heh**-ra-kleez
Herodotus	Heh-**rod**-ot-us
Hieron	Hee-**air**-on
Hippocrates	Hipp-**ok**-rat-eez
Iliad	**Ill**-ee-ad
Mycenae	My-**see**-nee
Odysseus	Od-**iss**-ee-us
Odyssey	**Od**-iss-eel
Orestes	Or-**est**-eez
Peloponnesian	Pel-op-on-**eez**-ee-un
Pericles	**Per**-ik-leez
Pheidias	**Fide**-ee-as
Plato	**Play**-toh
Pythagoras	Pie-**thag**-or-us
Roxana	Rocks-**ar**-na
Sappho	**Saf**-oh
Socrates	**Sok**-rat-eez
Solon	**Soh**-lon
Sophocles	**Sof**-ok-leez
Syracuse	**Sir**-a-kuse
Thales	**Thay**-leez
Zeus	Zy**oos**

Books to read

Ancient Greece by John Ellis Jones (Kingfisher, 1992)

Ancient Greece At A Glance by John Malam (Macdonald Young Books, 1998)

Eyewitness Guides: Ancient Greece by Anita Ganeri (Dorling Kindersley, 1993)

History Beneath Your Feet: Ancient Greece (Wayland, 1999)

History Makers: Ancient Greeks by Clare Chandler (Wayland, 1994)

Indiana Jones Explores Ancient Greece by John Malam (Evans Brothers, 1993)

Look Inside A Greek Theatre (Wayland, 1999)

The Ancient World: Greece by Robert Hull (Wayland, 1997)

The Greek News by Philip Steele and Anton Powell (Walker Books, 1996)

The Iliad by Ian Strachan (Kingfisher, 1997)

Websites

These sites provide excellent sources of information about all aspects of ancient Greek history, literature and people:

http://argos.evansville.edu
http://www.perseus.tufts.edu

Index